Town or Country?
A Victorian Dilemma

written by Ken Adey

illustrated by Shelagh McNicholas

Contents

Town or country?

By the early 1800s, hundreds of thousands of people were living and working in towns. A lot of new machinery had been invented. The first factories had opened. Many of the new machines in the factories were driven by steam power. To get the steam you had to burn coal so many new coal mines were opened. These factories and mines needed a lot of workers.

In the countryside there were not enough jobs for everybody. Many people decided to leave for the towns. They knew they would be able to get a job in a factory or mine. They knew that workers there were paid more money. There were jobs there for women and children as well. They knew that in the towns thousands of extra houses had been built quickly so that there was somewhere for the workers to live. They would have a home to go to.

It seemed that life in the town would be much better. There would be plenty of work, more money and a house to live in. But was it really better in the town?

Work in the town

Men, women and children worked in the factories. Most of these early factories were called **mills** and they made cloth.

Everyone worked for 12 or 14 hours a day, 6 days a week. Inside the mill it was very hot. It sometimes made it difficult to breathe. The **overseer**'s job was to make sure everybody worked hard. Some overseers were cruel and beat any child who was not working properly.

Children had to clean the machines while they were still working.

If they were not quick enough, they got tangled up in a machine they were trying to clean. Lots of children lost fingers, a hand or an arm. Some were so badly injured that they died.

"Any worker in the mill caught talking, whistling or singing will be fined 6d (2½ pence)."

Working in a coal mine was probably even worse. Men used pick axes and shovels to dig out the coal. Women and children dragged carts full of coal or carried it in baskets on their back. Sometimes the tunnels were so narrow that you had to crawl on your hands and knees.

Mines were dangerous. There was a lot of gas underground. Sometimes it choked the miners to death. The flame from a candle or a spark from a pick axe could make the gas explode. Tunnels often collapsed and buried the miners alive.

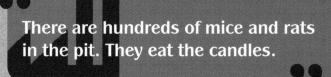

> There are hundreds of mice and rats in the pit. They eat the candles.

A mine worker's day:

5 am: Get up and walk to work

6 am: Start work

8 am: Breakfast (30 minutes rest)

12 am: Lunch (60 minutes rest)

7.30 pm: Finish work and walk back home

> At 6.30 am there was a terrific explosion. It shook the ground for miles around. When we were able to go into the mine, we found 14 men and boys dead.

Work in the country

Farm workers also worked for at least 12 hours a day.
At harvest time you had to work until 8 or 9 pm.
Most women and children did not work all the time.
They worked only at very busy times, like **harvest** time.

"
Harvesting is hard work. The straw cuts into your hands and scratches your arms. Working all day in the hot sun can make you feel dizzy and sick.
"

> Snowy winter mornings are the worst. I have to climb up an icy ladder on to the haystack to cut away a large bundle of hay. Then I carry it on my shoulders for half a mile across the fields and feed it to the cows. Sometimes I have to do this 3 or 4 times before there is enough for all the cows.

The work was hard but there were different jobs to be done at different times of the year.

Most of the time there was nobody watching over you. You could stop from time to time for a break. Men always took some beer with them when they went to work in the fields because it was thirsty work.

Lunch time for the farm workers was a time to relax.

"I watched the women hoeing the field. They seemed to work for 3 or 4 minutes and then stop to talk or call to someone passing by in the lane."

Sometimes my wife works on the farm. If the weather is good she puts the baby to sleep in a box filled with hay at the edge of the field. If the weather is bad, one of our other children has to stay at home to look after him.

Living in the town

Workers' houses were built in long rows, back to back. Many families had only enough money to rent one room in the house. If this was a room at the back of the house you had no window. This was your home. This was where you cooked, ate and slept.

A slum in 19th century London.

"The first room I went into had no windows. A woman and 4 children lived there. There was no furniture at all. The room next door had one small window but there were 10 people living here."

Sometimes 8 or more people lived in one room. The rooms were dark, dirty, cold and damp. The worst room to live in was the cellar. There was often water on the floor that had come in from the street above.

Fact

The lavatory pits often became full and overflowed. The waste ran down the gutters in the street and even got into the cellars of the houses.

The water pump often breaks down. Then we have to fetch water from a well over a quarter of a mile away. Water carriers do come down the street selling water but we can never afford it.

There were no water taps in the house. You had to fetch water from a pump in the street and the water was not very clean. It was used for cooking and making tea. Often there was not enough to waste it on washing your clothes or yourself.

The only lavatory was at the end of a long row of houses. It was really just a large pit in the ground covered by a small wooden shed. There was often one lavatory being used by over 200 people.

Fact

Workmen came to clear out the lavatory. They dug the waste out of the pit and carried it away in carts. Because the smell was so bad they usually did this during the night.

Living in the country

" Some of the houses we came to were in a very poor state. The thatch had holes in and there were weeds growing in it. Many of the windows were cracked or broken. "

The house of a farm worker often looked small but quite attractive from the outside, especially if it had a **thatched** roof. It was not so nice when you looked inside. Most houses had two very small rooms. You lived in one and slept in the other. The floor was just earth. These houses were very cold in the winter. The thatched roof often leaked when it rained.

Families were large and often 8 or 10 people lived in these tiny houses. There was some wooden furniture. Most would have some chairs, stools and a table. There was a fireplace at one end of the room. Because the room was so small, there was often no need to light a candle or lantern at night. You could see well enough by firelight.

Mud floors were not so bad in the summer but in winter they soon became damp and slimy.

The inside of a farm worker's house was very basic; it was damp and dirty.

Outside there was a garden that was used to grow vegetables and fruit. At the bottom of the garden was the lavatory. Like those in the towns this was really only a hole in the ground, but at least you did not have to share it with other families.

Fact

When it was time to empty the lavatory you had to make sure your doors and windows were tightly shut. But there was no way to stop the smell coming down the chimney!

Fact

The floor was often lower than the ground outside, so the water would often run in when it rained.

Rainwater was collected in a barrel against the wall of the house. If that water ran out there was usually a well nearby that you could use.

Health in the town

If you were a worker in a town in the early 1800s there was a very good chance that you would die before you were 20 years old. Out of every 100 children born, over twenty died before their first birthday. You lived and worked in dirty conditions. The water you drank was not clean. Men drank a lot of beer instead. This was not very good for you either.

Fact

The smell inside many of the houses in hot weather was terrible. Doctors who visited could stay in the house for only a short time before rushing outside to be sick.

Fact

Everybody worked so hard that they needed as much sleep as possible. To stop babies crying during the night, mothers often gave them a drug called **opium** to make them sleep. If you gave the baby too much it never woke up again!

The streets were filthy. They were full of waste from the lavatories. People threw rotten food out into the street. Dogs roamed about. There was no fresh air anywhere.

Street sellers in London sold food such as bread and potatoes to the poor.

You probably ate quite a lot but the food you ate was not good for you. You ate the food that was cheap to buy.

In London even the poorest worker often gets meat, and always gets bread, cheese and beer for his meals.

Cholera was sometimes called "the black illness" because it turned your skin and fingernails black.

This cartoon shows how dirty the rivers were. Cholera and typhoid were spread through dirty water.

Diseases killed people everyday.
Smallpox killed thousands of people every year. **Tuberculosis** attacked your lungs and it spread easily in the crowded houses.
Typhoid was caught from dirty water. Then in the 1830s a new killer illness appeared in the towns. This was called **cholera**.

Health in the country

If you were a worker in the country in the early 1800s you could expect to live longer than a town worker. There was a good chance that you would live to be 40 or even older.

The inside of your house might be crowded but outside things were not so bad. You had your own lavatory. The lavatories did not overflow into the street. You had clean water to drink. You worked in the open air all year round.

The fresh air made the country a much healthier place to live than the industrial town.

You bought less food because you had less money, but you did not have to buy all of your food. You had your own garden where you grew fresh vegetables and fruit. You were able to buy milk from the farm.

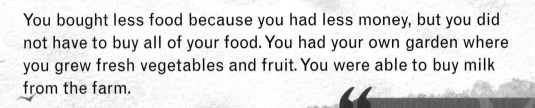

> We could buy milk from the farm for a penny a jug. It didn't matter how big your jug was, they still filled it right up for a penny.

The garden had trees of every sort. There were apples, pears, damsons and plums. Under the trees were gooseberry bushes, raspberries and currants. The rest of the garden was divided into strips growing potatoes, lettuce, cabbage, onions, radishes and parsnips.

You ate very little meat but you would have bacon. Many families kept a pig in a sty in the garden. When the pig was fat enough it was killed. The bacon would be salted to make sure it did not go bad. This would provide food for the family for many months.

You could catch the same diseases that town workers caught, but you were not likely to catch cholera. Working outside in all weathers gave many people **rheumatism**.

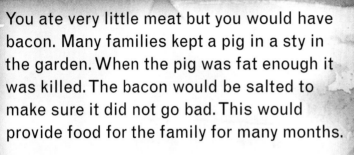

> When a pig was killed it was always done at night. My dad said it was bad luck to kill a pig in daylight. I never knew why.

Rheumatism caused many farm workers to have bad backs and aching joints.

I watched him digging a ditch. He had rheumatism badly in his knees. They were very swollen and it was painful. But he still went to work each day and did the same jobs he had always done.

Which was the best?

Life was difficult for working people wherever they lived. If you worked in the countryside you were paid less money. Women and children could only get work on the farms at very busy times. In the towns everybody in the family could go to work and earn money.

Wherever you lived you worked lots of hours each day for 6 days a week. But in the country you could have a rest or a drink if you wanted. There was also much less chance of being hurt or killed on a farm than in a factory or coal mine.

In the town you had to use a lot of your money to buy enough food. In the country you were able to grow a lot of your own food. But this meant more work to do in your garden. If you didn't do this you would soon have very little food to eat.

Wherever you lived your house was very crowded. None of the houses was very comfortable. None of the houses had much furniture. But in the country your small house was your own. Your family also had a lavatory all to itself!

In the towns the streets were dirty and smelly. In the country you went out of your house into the fresh air. Children in the towns had nowhere to play except in the streets. In the country they had the lanes and the fields for play.

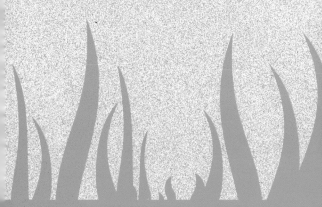

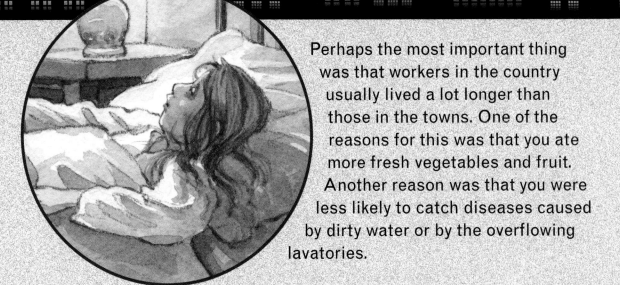

Perhaps the most important thing was that workers in the country usually lived a lot longer than those in the towns. One of the reasons for this was that you ate more fresh vegetables and fruit. Another reason was that you were less likely to catch diseases caused by dirty water or by the overflowing lavatories.

Wherever you lived life was hard but perhaps you agree that life in the country was the best?

Glossary

cholera disease caused by poor quality drinking water

harvest time when crops are picked

mill factory where thread was woven into cloth

opium drug which makes you sleepy

overseer man who made sure factory workers worked hard

rheumatism illness affecting the joints such as your knees
  or fingers – the joint swells and becomes stiff and painful

smallpox disease causing fever and skin sores

thatched made of straw

tuberculosis lung disease

typhoid disease often caused by dirty milk

Index